SERICULTURAL ECONOMICS

SERICULTURAL ECONOMICS

T. SUBRAMANI

SERIALS PUBLICATIONS
NEW DELHI (INDIA)

First Published – 2008

ISBN: 978-81-8387-204-1

Published by

SERIALS PUBLICATIONS
4830/24, Prahlad Street, Ansari Road
Darya Ganj, New Delhi-110002 (India)
Phone : 23245225 Fax : 91-11-23272135
E-mail: serials@satyam.net.in

Contents

budding scholar with appreciable research aptitude. He has contributed few articles in the reputed journals and seminar proceedings. I hope this book will help the research scholars those work on rural economics. I wish him all the success in his venture.

Date: 30.12.2007

E. Marimuthu
Head of the Department of Economics
Arignar Anna Govt. Arts College,
Cheyyar-604 407, Thiruvannamalai Dt.

Foreword

The book entitled *"Sericultural Economics"* provides a fairly comprehensive description and analysis of the development of economic through sericulture. Generally Speaking History of Sericulture has been very clearly portrayed in the book. While analyzing in depth of the book it speaks of the problems faced by sericulture farmers and their Socio, Economic status very vividly in the fourth chapter of the book. How the government machinery is taking care on the sericulture farmers especially providing Housing Facilities through TAHDCO in order to improve their housing condition has been thoroughly examined. This book also very interestingly highlights how sericulture provides employment opportunities to the rural people particularly womenfolk, a boost to the job seekers as it encourages the self employment. The author has suggested the wasteland may be used for the sericulture, which needs support in a wider ranger. The author has seriously concentrated on the subjects on which he has tried to work without any lapse to some extent though it seems maiden attempt.

Mr. T. Subramani, Hailing from poor agricultural family in a villages near Arcot, Vellore District of Tamilnadu with sound knowledge in the subjects of Economics, is working as a guest faculty in the Department of Economics Muthurangam Govt. Arts College, Vellore at present. He has also served in the Department of Economics. Arignar Anna Govt. Arts College, Cheyyar for sometimes. He is very enthusiastic young and energetic

Acknowledgement

I wish to express my most sincere and profound gratitude to Dr. M. Naganath M.A., Ph.D former professors and Head Department of Economics, University of Madras, Deputy Chairman of the State Planning Commission, Tamilnadu.

I owe a lot of gratitude to Dr. Ravinthirakumar M.A., M.Phil., Ph.D, Reader (Rtd..) in Economics Muthurangam Government Arts College, Vellore.

I am indebted to Dr. E. Marimuthu, M.A. (His) M.A. (Tamil), M.A. (HR), M.A. (ENG) M.Phil., Ph.D Reader in History, A.A. Govt. Arts College, Cheyyar.

I also wishes to record my grateful thanks to Dr. N. Radhakrishnan, M.A., M.Phil., Ph.D Senior Selection Grade Lecturer in Economics, MGAC, Vellore.

I am grateful to my Grand Mother Late Poongili Ammal, My Sister Late T. Sarala, My Father and Mother and sincere thanks to My all family Memebers.

Finally wish to acknowledge my thanks to Serials Publications New Delhi.

T. Subramani

1

Introduction

In developing countries like India, agriculture and agro-based industries play a vital role in the improvement of rural economy. The limited availability of land, the limited cash returns and agriculture being confined to one or two seasons in the year, have made villages to look for supporting rural industries such as sericulture. Agriculture and sericulture are adopted simultaneously by the agriculturists in regions where the ecological conditions are favorable. In India over three million people are employed in various fields of sericulture. It is a Agro-based cottage industry and provides sample work for the women folk in the rural areas in rearing silkworms, while the male members work in the fields. The sericulture industry is now practiced as a main profession and as a major cash crop of the country.[1]

Historically, sericulture was introduced for the first time, in china by Hoshomin the queen of china. For a long time sericulture was considered to be a national secret by the Chinese government and as an industry it was not known in other countries. Later it was introduced into Europe and Japan as well. According the reports available, sericulture was introduced into India about 400 Years back and the industry flourished as an agro industry till 1857 with an annual production of two million pounds of silk fibre. The Industry survived the onslaught of the perbine disease during the period from 1857 to 1895. However, after 1928, the sericulture industry showed a decline in its production owing to the fierce competition from advanced sericultural countries such as Japan, China and European Countries. After Independence the industry is flourishing as an agro industry giving employment to over 3.5 Million People in the country.[2]

Sericulture

In strict sense "Sericulture" would refer the processes involved in production of natural silk "Serio" is a latin word meaning silk. Silk is a natural filament created by the silkworm. Therefore, sericulture means the raising or rearing of silk worm for production of silk. Sericulture refers to cultivation of mulberry and rearing of silk worm for harvesting natural silk. It is highly labour intensive and profitable venture and therefore suits well to labour rich countries like India.

Types of Natural Silk (Sericulture)

There are four types of natural silk, viz., (i) Mulberry Silk, (ii) Tasar Silk, (iii) Eri Silk, (iv) Muga Silk. India is the only country in the world which produces all the above four types because favorable agro-climatic conditions.

Non–Mulberry Silk

The three other kinds of silk are called non-mulberry silk as mulberry is not the food plant here. These are also called wild silk since the worms are not fully domesticated as mulberry worms and are practiced in forest and hilly areas. Mostly by tribals nearly eighty insects are known to produce wild silk of more or less economic values of them about a dozen are of importance in India. The non-mulberry silk are Tasar Silk Eri Silk, Muga Silk.

An attempt is made in the following pages to describes how mulberry sericulture is practiced. The practices in the states of Andhra, Karnataka and Tamil Nadu are very similar. Mulberry sericulture can be distinctly divided into four operations as follows:

(a) Mulberry Cultivation

(b) Silkworm rearing

(c) Disposal of Cocoons, and

(d) Silkworm egg Production

Mulberry Cultivations

Mulberry Cultivation is purely an agricultural operation and a major factor determining quantity of production and hence the profitability of sericulture. It is the major cost factor and time and labour consuming activity though less skilled as compared to silkworm rearing.

Mulberry is a hard plant capable of thriving under a variety of agro climatic conditions. It responds very well to good cultivation and optimum agriculture inputs and care. Depending upon the quality and efficiency of the operations, the lead yield varies enormously. Mulberry can be grown as bush, high bush, medium tree or long tree. Bust type is widely grown in south India. Which grows to a height of 5' to 7' and lasts for about 15 years. Within 4 to 5 months of plantation under irrigated conditions the plant grows to normal size and is ready for harvesting. As it is a pernnial plant it needs regular manual attention throughout the year.

Silk Worm

Silkworm rearing is a cottage activity carried by the sericulture in his own house or in a separate room build for this purpose. It is the second major activity in sericulture requiring lot of manual attention and becomes a complicated process when various technical and scientific aspects are to be understood and implemented for high productivity. It demands a substantial amount of managerial skill on the part of the rearers and his own experience forms a good guide.

Disposal of Cocoons

Disposal of cocoons is a major activity but the Sericulturist faces considerable difficulties in disposing of his cocoons. The disposal is bound by time factor as moths would emerge out of the cocoons after a certain time rendering the cocoons useless. The cocoons are sold at various Government and private marketing yards and sometimes to middlemen and commissions agents.

Production of Silkworm Eggs

Production of silkworm eggs is a precarious activity and the seed organization plays a vital role on which the success of the industry depends. The layings are called Disease free layings since care has to be taken, that the layings are healthy and free from any disease or infection after a microscope test. The establishment where the laying are produced is called a grainage.

Normally the type of laying used by the rearers is a cross breed layings produced from the Multivoltine Male Local Race (LR) and the Bivoltine Female Foreign Race. (FR)[3] . The FR and LR, DFLs are also called basic seed and are produced by Government grainages in their respective grainages. These DFLs are supplied to notification rearers for further multiplicatiob. These rearers breed the DFLs and sell the resultant seed cocoons to the government grainages. In the CB (Cross Breed) grainages the commercial seed is produced by cross breeding.

Mulberry sericulture is carried on a large scale. Therefore its activities are more systematized and organized as compared to the non mulberry sericulture activities.

By Products of Sericulture

Some by products emerge in the process of sericulture which are useful in various ways. Mulberry leaves and shoots left by the silkworm form good fodder to the cattle with marketed increase in milk yield. Castor plantation also yields castor seed for oil extraction. The oil cakes from about 60 Per cent of total weight with 4.5 per cent of nitrogen content. It is good antidote to white ants. Castor oil has soap, medicines, lubricants etc. It has a ready market. Live Eri pupae are consumed by the tribals. Dead pupae got after reeling are rich in protein and oil content. The oil is extracted and used for soap manufacture. Protein powder can be utilized in baking industries. It forms a rich feed for poultry, fishery and piggery. The silkworm excretes can be used as manure.

The rational utilization and disposal of by products helps the Seri culturist in further enhancing his economic gains.

Sericulture Activities in Chronology

Raising Mulberry Plantation

Mulberry plant being the sole food plant for the Bombyx Mori silk worms, cultivation of sufficient acerage of mulberry plantation is the pre-requiste of the sericultural activity.

Procurement of Silkworm Layings

In order to rear the silkworm, the required number of silk-worm eggs are made available from the Government Grainages. The suitability of seeds intented for a particular area shall be pre-decided viz. Univoltine, bivoltine and multivoltitle with specific race.

Hatching of Eggs

According to the hatching schedule, eggs are hatched either by using incubation or by natural process.

Chawki Rearing (Rearing of Young Silkworm)

Young Silkworms being sensitive, needs greatest care, stabilized environmental conditions, besides the nutritional part. Hence Chawki rearing centers are available to the farmers in the sericultural area, wherein the silkworm are reared up to the second moult in a conditioned atmosphere and supplied to the farmers.

Silkworm Rearing

Silkworms are reared in hygienic rearing houses during which the silkworms are fed on Mulberry leaves, Being a voracious eater, silkworm needs more mulberry leaves during its fourth and fifth stage. At the end of its fifth stage the worm eating and enters its pupal stage for which the full grown worm spins its protective cover known as cocoon. It takes 26-28 days for the young worm to grow up to spinning of cocoon.

Harvesting of Cocoons

Fully built cocoons are collected from the mount–ages or Chandrikas.

Stiffing

The green cocoons are dried and stifled to kill its pupae to prevent it from emerging in the form of butterfly, before they are stored.

Boiling or cooking

Cooking of cocoons is done to loosen the filaments in the cocoon and make it suitable for reeling. Cooking is preparatory to reeling.

Reeling

The Process of unwinding the filaments from silk cocoons using charka or any other improvised reeling machine is known as reeling. The silk is known by its reeling mechanism adopted for the reeling viz. Charka silk, filature silk, etc.

Re-reeling or Winding

Reeled silk yarn is again re-reeled in suitable machines to maker it into different forms of carriages viz. skeins, lanks, bobbins etc. Re-reeling also controls the denier and uniformity.

Throwing

Throwing is a process of doubling and twisting the silk yarn to make it stronger to withstand the stress and strain of the weaving process.

Weaving

Fabrics are woven on suitable designs using silk yarm in warp weft. A wide range of silk fabrics are woven using different weaving mechanisms viz. Handloom, Jacwuard, dobby-loom, pit-loom and power looms.

Processing

These woven fabrics are subjected to various process in order to dress up the fabric for a better look and finish. The common processes are degumming scouring, bleaching, weighting dyeing and printing and finishing.

Marketing

The processed fabrics are ready for marketing. Natural Silk fabrics always processes a great demand either in domestics market or for export.

The Central Silk Board

The cent ral silk board (C.S.B.) is a statuary body presently under the administrative control of the ministry of commerce. Government of India one of the earliest Commodity Boards. Constituted in April 1949 under the act of parliament (Act No. LXI of 1948) the CSB is an autonomous body triennially constituted with 36 members including the chairman and comprising of representatives drawn from both Houses of Parliament sericultural states and special inteest concerning the industry and trade.

The main functions of the Board are as follows:

1. The promoting the development of silk industry by such measure as it thinks best.
2. Understanding, assisting and encouraging scientific, Technological and economic research.
3. Collection of statistics.
4. Advising the Central Government on all matters relating to the development of Silk Industry.

The Import of raw silk and export of silk fabrics silk waste etc.

The board has its headquaters in Banglore with five regional offices in different regions for purpose of ensuring close coordination of central and state efforts to develop the sericulture industry. These are located at Banglore, Culcutta, New Delhi, Srinagar and Bombay.[4]

Silk Industry: A Tool for Women Employment

In the present system of male headed family women are serving mostly as voiceless workers. This is true in silk industry also silk industry has immense potentially to generate employment including women in rural areas and thus the industry is patronized both by central as well state level governments to popularize among people of rural cross sections.[5] A large number of women are engages in a variety of self employment schemes and handicrafts and sericulture is also one such self-employment avenue facilitating the women to improve their economic situation to a considerable extent.[6]

Sericulture plays a important role in improving the economic conditions of rural poor. In India agriculture is the main occupation and sericulture being agro-based fits very well in India rural structure. It also has a Vast potential for generating income and employment opportunities for the rural masses in many ways.[7]

Because it is a labour intensive cottage industry, one acre of plantations generations five man years of direct employment annually in mulberry cultivation, Silk warm rearing, twisting, weaving and implement fabrication. The various activities are nor season bound but carried out throughout the years.[8]

Statement of the Problem

A manifold increase in agriculture are allied activities is the only answer to stabilize the country economy especially the rural economy sericulture has been identified as an item of high income and employment potentially with a proven record over the previous years in our country. The time is very conductive and favorable for the sericulture farmers and promises a glorious future for the coming decades Sericulture plays a predominant role in shaping the economic destiny of rural poor.

As an agro-based cottage industry sericulture fits very well in India's rural structure. Where agriculture continues to be the main occupation recognizing the significance of sericulture the government took a series of developmental measures to popularize it. As a result sericulture has come age and is now poised for a great leap forward.

Sericulture is a labour intensive, agro-based cottage industry ideally suited to a predominantly agricultural state like Tamil Nadu. The state has the vest potential for sericulture development, particularly in the Vellore District where climate conditions are suitable for sericulture development.

The development of sericulture in the sholinghur block of vellore district could be a largely attributed the TAHDCO schemes, that has been doing a commendable job of serving the small mulberry growers and assisting them to plant more acres of mulberry besides providing required financial and infrastructural facilities the cope with increased cocoon production. IN the following chapters an attempt has been made to discuss the development role of sericulture in sholinghur block of Walajapet taluk in Vellore District.

Scope of the Study

It may be stated that the development of the rural economy depends not only on the development of agriculture but also largely on the role of it's allied activities like sericulture, Dairying, Poultry, Fisheries, piggery, small scale and cottage industries.

Sericulture is one of the major agro-based industry which is generating more employment in rural areas. And it highly is labour intensive. Sholinghur block of walaja taluk in vellore district is agricultural oriented area. Its economic development largely lies on the developmental role of agricultural and allied activities. The scope for industries and agricultural allied activities is very less due to lack of infrastructural facilities.[9]

Agricultural being one of the growing activity in the Block. So it can be believed that the development of sericulture through effective programmes schemes and training programmes may make the block more developed. Therefore the study is entitled "Socio Economic Conditions of sericulture Farmers in Sholinghur Block. Vellore District is undertaken.

Objectives of the Study

1. The assess the socio-economic conditions of the sericulture farmers on Sholinghur Block, Vellore District.
2. To Study the cropping pattern of mulberry cultivation and sericulture farmings.
3. To evaluate the sustainable role of TAHDCO in sericulture farming in the study area.
4. To analysis how far the sericulture programme helpful in developing the rural economy.
5. To findout the problems and prospects in sericulture.

Hypothesis

1. There is a marked improvement in overall quality of life of the sericulture farmers.
2. There is a significant favourable climate for women and children in employment and income.

Methodology

The Methodology of the present study is described here. The following steps were taken in the present empirical study.

Nature of the Research Design

The research design of the study was "empirical and descriptive in character.

Nature of the Data Required

The objectives setforth in this study had necessitated the researcher to look for the data. It was an empirical and descriptive work and hence there was a need for the collective of date. Due to resource constraints, it was decided to concentrate mainly on the primary data.

Data and Selection of Samples

As the study was aiming at throw light on the overall working of the sericulture programme in the sholinghur Block of Walajapet taluk in Vellore District. There are 320 sericulture farmer in sholinghur Block. Due to simplification and other constraints 25 Per cent of the total cultivators i.e., 80 Cultivators have been selected in 10 villages at random in Sholinghur Block for the purpose of research work, The sholinghur Block has 47 inhabited villages, from this 47 Villages the following 10 Villages have been selected as the sample villages. They are (1) Keeraisathu, (2) K. M. Palayam (3) Melpadi, (4) Rendady (5) Permalakuppam (6) ponnai (7) Vallimalai (8) Melvenkettapuram (9) Thagarakuppam and (10) Paramasathu.

Apart from the sample size the Researcher had collected data and necessary information by discussion with officials of the sericulture Department, Technical Service Centre Walajapet, Office of the Deputy Director of Sericulture at Vellore, Regional Deputy Director of Sericulture at Sathuvachari, Vellore , Sholinghur Block Development Office and Sholinghur Agricultural Development Office. Some Secondary data were used in this study. The sources for secondary data was Action plan Reports of Sericulture Department.

Data Sheets

The Collected data had vast information and as such all of them were not required for the study. Inorder to cull out the necessary primary data from filled questionnaire, The researcher has prepared an elaborate and well structured Master Table. The data were converted into necessary sub-tables and they were modified after consultation with the Guide. Hence the data sheets were structured in nature and Character.

Processing and Consolidation of Data

The Collected Data were to be processed further and consolidated suitably for the purpose of analysis. The work was carried out during September 1999. Further "Master tables were also carefully prepared to put them in order so that they could be meaningfully used through formation of suitable tables for analysis and answering the objectives stated.

Analysis and Interpretation of the Data

The analysis was carried on by applying simple statistical tools like percentages, growth rate and averages, Besides suitable diagrammatic representation (Pie and Bar Diagram) were also made use of in this study,

Tools Used in this Study

Annual Growth Rate

$$= Y1 - Yo / Y1 \times 100$$

where

Y1 – Stands for the First year.

Yo – Stands for the immediately previous year.

Average

$$\Sigma N / n$$

Where

N = Total of the Observations

n = Number of Observation.

The Calculation were done by manually the results were carefully noted and they were interpreted rightly, keeping the stated objectives of the study in mind. The report was written in lucid languages and the same is given in the fourth chapter.'

Chapter Scheme

The First chapter deals with the general introduction of the study. Second Chapter committed to review of literature, profile of the study areas described in third chapter, socio-economic conditions of sericulture farmer is presented in the fourth chapter and fifth chapter ends up with summary and conclusion.

Notes and Reference

1. Hand Book of Agriculture (1997), The Indian Coucil of Agriculture Research, New Delhi, p. 1226.
2. *Ibid.*, p. 1225.
3. Economics of Sericulture and Silk Industry in India, p. 10.
4. Agriculture in India by (2000), AD, Khadhygramodyog, February 1997, p. 227.
5. Economics of Sericulture and Silk Industry in India, pp. 11 to 13.
6. *Ibid.*, p. 20.
7. Gupta B. K. and Gupta Y. K. (1997), "Silk Industry a Tool for Women Employment", India Farming-July, pp. 17-18.
8. Dr. V. Shobha, V. Vimala Devi and Jyothi (1998), "Socio Economic Status of Women in Sericulture", *Kurukshetra* June, pp. 46-47.
9. Arkady Leokum (1994), "Tell me Why", U.S.A., New York, pp. 364-365.

2

Review of Literature

Reviews of past studies would always be useful in Book, an attempt has been made by the Author towards this direction.

Sericulture plays a Predominant role in shapping the economic destint of the rural poor. As an agro-based cottage industry, sericulture fits very well in India's Rural structure, where agriculture continues to be the main occupation. In this chapter some of the past empirical, microlevel and macrolevel studies had been reviewed.

The handloom silk weaving industry is concentrated in the states of Tamil Nadu, Uttar Pradesh, West Bengal, Andhra Pradesh and Jammu and Kashmir. According to the villages and small scale industries committee prior to the introduction of planning there were 2 Lakhs looms on silk. The Total number of the looms engaged in silk weaving is 1,25,000 and power looms is 3,300. [1]

A study on Socio-Economic Status of women by shobha, Vimala Devi and Jhothi they examined nearly 215 families engaged in sericulture. A majority of BC & SC women in the sample revealed that poverty illiteracy, Indebtedness, Lack of skills and absence of other alternatives in the rural areas forced them to join the work force at an early age. The result of their study was, it is significant in the lower income group families earning of sample women range between Rs.5,000 and Rs. 10,000 per annum of whom SCs constitute about 43.5Per cent in the sample followed by BC consititute a back followed by FC respondents. However the sample woman engaged in sericulture earn income more than those dependent on agriculture. [2]

The all India Handlooms Board extents assistances to the silk cooperatives on the same basis as far cotton loans. At Present, a loan of Rs. 250 is given to each weaver to enable him to pay the share capital and become a number. This amount has to be repaid in four years. A Loan of Rs. 500/- is issued for each Loan towards the working capital to purchase furniture appliance etc. In 1973 out of 27,307 silk handlooms, 9,500 looms were covered by 40 Silk weavers co-operatives societies in Tamilnadu Silk handlooms weavers co-operatives societies numbering 65 with 15,999 looms were functioning in TamilNadu.[3]

Sericulture is a cottage industry with and agricultural base. "A Cottage industry is thus one which is carved on wholly or primarily with the help of members of the family either as a whole or a part time occupation".[4]

According to Gupta B. K. and Gupta Y. K. in the present system of male headed family women are serving mostly as voiceless workers. This is true industry silk industry has immense potentially to generalized employnment including human in rural areas and this the industry is favourised both by central as well state level governments to popularize among people of rural cross sections.[5]

Kshirsagar in his study entitled sericulture research in Maharastra. A Historical Perspective found that the races of Bombyx mori are much superior and commercially used in different agro climate regions of Maharastra. These races have been stabilized fully by their selective rearing through over 140 generations. Further multi-allocational trails will be necessary these encouraging results can lead to formulation of further research and extension programmed. The central silk board can extend its helping hand. The sericulture industry in Maharastra has a very bright road future.[6]

Mishat Waseem (1999) stated that with the launch of the sericulture projecr in Vidisha the yield has gone up to more than Rs. 15,000 to Rs 20,000 Per acre of land every year. "with better Technology", the yield can be improved and he concluded that with the launch of the sericulture project in vidisha, a district Madhya Pradesh the life Styles of the rural women undergone a metamorphosis.[7]

Shoba, Vimala and Jyothi (1999), in their empirical study revealed that a majority of human belonging to SC community were unable to spend money on education of their children. This is mainly due to the low paying capacity and lack cannot afford to send their childrens. It is a significant to observe that a majority of BCs own more land in the sample formulated by Ocs and SCs in the village. This indicated a change in the land ownership as compared to surrounding villages. But human do not own land in their names nor have they any wise and are in decision making with regard to marriage, education of their children and purchases of assests for the family or sale of produce.[8]

Joseph Sebatian has pointed out that the cost of labour of Kerala is much more than or other states. A few farmers who did depend entirely on rented labour for dcing sericulture felt unemotional. A few of them even contributed to a negative to a negative influence in our efforts of popularizing sericulture. We also see that those who are able to utilize the family the labour still find its impressive. Many farmers who started right from the beginning still continuing and also attracting others to take up sericulture. So after a period of initial confusion many are coming forward gradually to take up the promising Venture.[9]

Narusaiah and Kuberudu (1995), attempted to critically analyse the development of sericulture of Anantapur district of Royal Scheme region in Andhra Pradesh, they pointed out that spectacular development has taken place in sericulture in Anatapur district and now it has become a way of life to many small and mariginal farmers and others in the district providing direct and indirect employment with its forward and backward linkages. And concluded that sericulture would play a pivotal role in shapping the economy, providing lucrative in come and employment.[10]

Nylekumar (1995) in a study entitled "A review of Sericulture programmes undertaken by Malanadu Development Society-Kerala". Noted that the importances that is now attached to sericulture is evident from the fact that government itself has actively come into the picture. It is providing incentives to extend mulberry cultivation on 50,000 acres over the five years. A very encouraging development is that the government through the Khadi and village industries Board, has started purchasing cocoons from farmers. It should be possible to the highest class for processing cocoons, spinning, reeling, weaving and printing etc. The aim should he to establish a high trading image for Kerala Silk. In other states there is the tradition a centuries. But we have their expensive to draw in the newcomers here can gain efforts made by the pioneers in the cooperative movement and they stand to suffer losses if sufficient facilities are located." [11]

Dolli made an empirical study to know the impact of training on knowledge and yield among sericulturist in Hashan, Kolar and Banglore districts of Karnataka, He observed that gain in knowledge of trained sericulturists was higher with respect to all practices compared to untrained sericulturists and knowledge about silkworm rearing practices were better than mulberry cultivation. Among all training programmes, knowledge level was higher in case of CSB 45 Central Silk Board Followed by CSB 60 DOS 10 and DOS 30.

Further he concluded that the coverage of mulberry cultivation and silkworm rearing was good while that of post cocoon technology was poor, The use of extension teaching methods in all training programmes was inadequate.[12]

Krishnana state that success of sericulture as a viable crop. Largely depends on the production of mulberry leaf and its conversion to cocoons at economic costs, He listed some of the problems those are:

1. Lack of training to selected beneficiaries who are taking up this activity for the first time.
2. Lack of Timely credit by bankers.
3. Lack of adequate infrastructure facilities mainly for marketing,
4. Delay in release of Subsidy.
5. Lack of proper monitoring results in the mis-utilization of funds, And his conclusion was the implementation of world bank aided sericulture project I and II has helped in the creation of the necessary infrastructure like technical service centers. Establishment of grainages for supplying dfts, Governemnt Silk farms cocoons markert reeling units etc., In view of this a potential exists for financing 48,000 ha Mulberry Cultivation in the tradition and non traditional areas during the VIII plan period on 2,12,000 ha. In the long run.[13]

Kshrisagar stated that the experiments of new races of Bombyx mori the mulberry silk worm i.e wai 1 and wai 4, in maharastra these experiments of course were very much successful and these two races were assessed for their performance taking into consideration 15 parameter (Qualitive and quantitative) and now their multilocational trails are intended and they have fortunately been taken up by BAIF. These encouraging results led to formulation of further research and extension programmes. It is however a little unfortunate that the pace of progress is not to the expectation because of various constraints in their actual implementation, further he pointed out that in the future, grainages for seed organization programmes should be taken up for bivoltine and multivoltine races. Bivoltiner could be confined to the western Ghats were the altitude ranges from 3000 to 4000 ft and for post harvest technology also and for read weaving also and of course this should include trainings which are taken up by the Khadi and village industries Board If NGOs come forward and establish such research stations for their local geographical needs that will be very much fruitful.[14]

Rao and Hanumappa brings out the variation in the socio-economic and agro climatic factors which are responsible for the differential rates of performance of the mulberry cultivation and the cocoon production while Thimmaiah and Rao infer that by and large the new programmes of sericulture and benefiting mostly the well to do farmers rather than their poor counterparts, Hanumappa's study shows that this is mainly due to certain economic enjoyed by the large farmers as compared to the small farmers.[15]

Hanumappa's study shows that sericulture has vast employment generating capacity both on farm and off-farm. His exercise is restricted to mulberry cultivation and cocoon rearing which even though shows some regional variation has great employment potential. He Pleads for taking up sericulture development activities on a much larger scale in the state as a means also of generating higher levels of employment in the rural areas.[16]

Thimmiah and Rao indicate that poor extension services could be one of the major reasons for the failure of bivoltine programmes and for the differential impact on farmers. According to them big farmers have by and large benefited most from this programme. The landless and the poor farmers have derived in direct benefits from sericulture through its high employment potential. The middle level farmers who are engaged in, have however, attained economic viability.

It is held that most of the sericulturists are aware of the economic advantages of the bivoltine rearings. But certain handicaps like lack of rearing houses, irrigation etc., are mainly responsible for the slow growth of bivoltine variety in the sate. Hence they recommend that to achive breakthrough apart from helping the farmers to have separate rearing houses. It is necessary to make substantial investments in well irrigation in the rainfed region and in new region to create a number of incetives with a view to inducing more farmers to take up sericulture. Further reeling activity should be encourages in the non traditional areas in order to create sufficient demand for the cocoons produced in these areas. To solve some of these problems the authors recommend the establishment of governement-owned silk farms, grainages and cocoon markets.[17]

Girippa and Govindaraju have found out on the basis of their study of sericulture households that certain diseases like Flacherie, Graserie and Muscardine affect the cocoon yields in varying degrees depending on the varieties reared. Their study show that the local varieties have greater resistence to disease than the rest. The cross breed and bivoltine varieties seem to be more sensitive and the authors notice a higher incidence of diseases in these cases are compared to local variety. However there are variations in the extent of incidence of disease on cocoon yields across different agro-climatic regions within the state. An effective control of the diseases incidence-preventive and curative through extension agencies will help in bridging the gap between the targeted and the actual growth. A suggestion which can be considered in this regard is about formulating insurance system which covers the risks due to the incidence of diseases.[18]

Nagaraja Rao presents in this study the official account of the sericulture extension activities in the state. He outlines the objectives and the modes operandi of different sericulture extension agencies. According to Nagaraja Rao under Karnataka sericulture project KSP. The extension agencies have been in a position to improve the extension methodology and the techniques of rearing which may goa long way in achieving the targeted production of 6,500 metric tons of silk by the end of the seventh plan. In addition to highlighting the importance of adopting improved and effective extension methods. The author provides several policy guidelines for the overall development of sericulture in the state.[19]

According to Koshy natural silk has been identified as an item of high export potentially with an annual growth rate of about 30 per cent over the previous year. The country is all set to achieve a protracted target of Rs. 1000 crores per annum towards the end of VIII plan period from natural silk exports. The time is very conductive and favorable for the Indian Silk exports. The time is very conductive and favourable for the India silk exporters and promises a glorious future for the coming decades. At a time when the world demand for silk is growing high, the traditional silk producing countries like Japan, Korea, Brazil and Russia have drastically cut their production. Leaving India a wise scope for a massive increase in silk production and export. [20]

Notes and Reference

1. *Times of India* Year Book–1971.
2. Role of Rural Human in Sericulture the Staff of the Department of Sericulture Government of Karnataka Banglore, 1983, p. 5.
3. Handlooms Census of 1973.
4. S. S. Perumalswamy, "Economic Development of Tamil Nadu "Chand & Company Ltd., Ram Nagar, New Delhi, p. 188
5. Ghupta B. K. and Gupta Y. K. (1997), Silk Industry: A Tool for Women Employment", *Indian Farming,* July, p.17
6. Kshirsagar, K. K. "Sericulture Research in Maharastra A Historical Perpestive", Sericulture in India, p. 105.
7. Nishant Waseem (1999), "Silk Rule to Success", *Down to Earth*", March 15, p. 47.
8. Shobha, Vimala and Jyothi (1995), "Weaving A Silken Future", "*Social Welfare*", June , pp. 29 to 30.
9. Joseph Sebastin, "Serviculture Promotion Programme of Avard, Chalakudy, Sericulture in India", Avard, Kerala p. 109.
10. Narasiah and Kuberudu (1995), "Sericulture–A Boon to Rural Poor 1", *Kurushetr*, May-June, pp. 64-65.
11. Nylekumar S. (1995), " A Review of Sericulture Programmes Undertaken by Programmes Undertaken by Muknadu Development Socity–Kerala", pp. 103 to 188.

12. Dolli S. S., "Impact of Training on Women Sericulturists: An Abstract" Central Sericultural Research and Training Institute, Mysore Sericultural in India, p. 121.

13. Krishnan N., Dy Manager NABARD "Operational Experience of Institutional Credit Support for Sericulture Programmes" Sericilture in Inida pp. 127,130.

14. Kshirasagar K. K. Retired Scientist, Pune , ' Sericulture in Maharastra–A Historical Perspective", Sericulture in India, p. 136.

15. Rao V. M. Hanumappa H. G and Thummaiah, "Sericulture for Rural Development, Himalaya Publishing, New Delhi, p. 8.

16. Hanumappa H. G. "Mulberry Cultivation, Cocoon Production and Employment Generation in Karnataka" Sericulture Culture for Rural Development Himalaya Publishing, New Delhi, pp. 126 to 149.

17. *Ibid.*, p. 153.

18. Girippa. S and Govindaraju. K. V., "Incidence of Disease and Yield Variations in Cocoon Production", Sericulture for Rural Development Himalaya Publishing, New Delhi, pp. 47-157.

19. Nagaraja Rao H. A. " The Official Account of Sericulture Extension Activities in Karnataka State", Sericulture for Rural Development, Himalaya Publishng, New Delhi, pp. 76 to 86.

20. Koshy T. D., "Silk Export and Development", Ashish Publishing House, New Delhi, p. 10.

3

Profile of the Study Area

The present newly formed "Vellore" District was carved out from erstwhile "North Arcot Ambedhkar District" in the same "Bharatratna" Babha Saheb Dr. B.R. Ambedkar. Many Splendoured personality of Dr. B.R. Ambedkhar a great scholar was an original thinker, writer, orator, debator, a great jurist and constitutionalist. Above all he was a restless, agitator and revolutionary, working for social reforms and radical social changes in our country.

Location and Area of Vellore District

The District is bounded on the north by the Chitoor district of Andhra Pradesh a portion of Chengalpattu district and on the south by Thriuvannamalai district on the west are district of dharmapuri and chitoot (Andhra Pradesh) while chengalpattu Kanchipuram district are in its the eastern boundary. The district is in the inland region and is of regular shape.

Total area of the district is 6077 Sq kms.. Head quarters of this district is vellore. The study are of sholinghur block is located with in this district.[1]

Population

Total population of the district is 3026432 persons as per 1991 census. Comprising of 1529944 males and 1496488 females. Rural population of the district is 2066718 persons (1048055 Males and 1018663 females) and urban population is 959714 persons. (481889 males and 477825 females).

The Scheduled caste and scheduled tribes population of the district, according to 1991 census, is 627318 and 49857 respectively. The rural urban break up of these population is indicated below.

Table 1
Details of Population in Vellore District

Details	*SC*	*ST*	*Total*	*Total (General of the District)*
Rural	480029 (91.20)	46311 (8.80)	526340 (100)	2066718
Urban	147289 (97.65)	3546 (2.35)	150835 (100)	959714
Total	627318 (20.73)	49857 (1.65)	677175 (22.38)	3026432

Source: 1991 Census Report.
Note: 1. Figures in brackets represent row–wise percentages to total.
2. Indicates percentages of SC/ST to total general Population of the district.

Languages and Religion

Main Languages spoken in the district are Tamil, Kannada, Marathi, Telugu and Urdu. Religion-wise breakup population of the district is indicated below as per 1991 census.

Hindus : The total Hindus are 2667424 persons and comprising 1349712 male and 1317712 female

Christians : The total Christian are70652 persons comprising 34932 male and 35720 female.

Muslim : The total muslims are 284610 persons, comprising 143099 male and 141511 female.

Jains	:	The total jains are 2872 persons comprising 1498 male and 1374 female
Sikhs	:	The total Sikhs are 370 persons comprising 242 male and 128 female
Buddhists	:	The total Buddhists are 37 persons comprising 23 male and 14 female
Other religion and pesuasion	:	32 male and 21
Female religion nor stated	:	406 Male and 8 Female

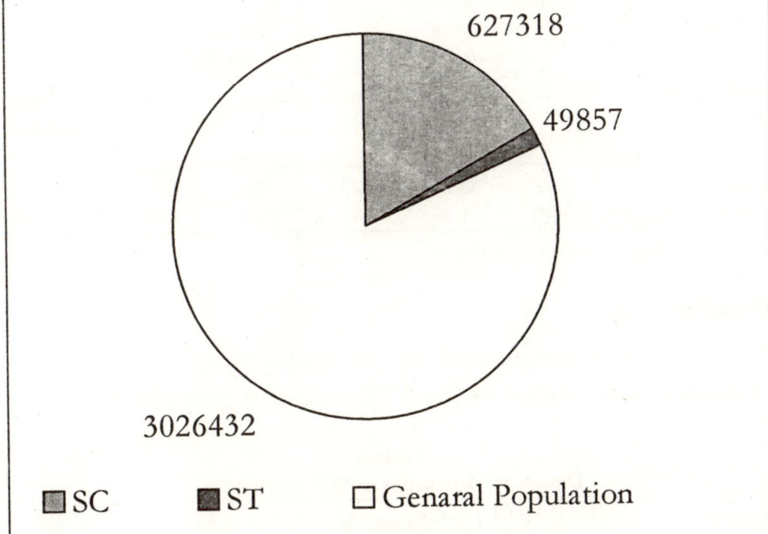

Figure 1: Details of Population in Vellore District

Rivers, Canals and Waterways

The district has the following important rives, Palar, South Pennar, the cheyyar and Ponnai, Barring a few days in the rain season, these rivers are mostly dry and sandy wastes.

Towns, Villages and Amenities

The district is at present consists of 7 taluks and 20 community development blocks. It has32 towns and 906 villages (808 in habitel villages and 98 uninhabited villages).

The urban population of the district as percentage of total population I the census years 1981 and 1991 is indicated below. It also shows the sex ratio and density of population (per sq. km) in the urban areas of the district in relation to state.

Table 2
Details of Urban Population in Vellore and Tamilnadu

State/District	*Urban population as percentage of total population*		*Sex ratio 1991 (Females per 1000 Males)*			*Density population per sq. km*
	1981	*1991*	*Total*	*Rural*	*Urban*	
Tamilnadu	32.95	34.20	972	983	951	428
Vellore (N.A.A.Dt)	30.80	31.76	987	984	992	494

Source: Encyclopaedic District Gazette.

Amenities

Number (with Percentage) of villages having one are more amenities in the district as per 1991 census is given below.

Table 3
Details of Amenities in Vellore District

Amenities	*Number of inhabited Villages*	*Percentages*
Education	759	93.94
Medical	322	39.85
Drinking Water	808	99.88
Post and Telegraph	519	64.23
Market/Hat	121	14.98
Communications	689	85.27
Approach by pucca road	639	79.08
Power supply	805	99.63

Source: Encyclopaedic District Gazette.

Agriculture and Irrigation

Cultivation is the mainstay of the people of the district and the rural economy centers round agriculture. The district is dependent on seasonal rain for successful agricultural operations. Some of the taluks in particular which enjoy irrigation facilities like vellore is known for its substantial contribution to the agricultural production of the district tanks and wells are the chief sources of irrigation and there are enough supplies in them when monsoons occur normally. During year of monsoon failure, drought conditions prevail and productivity is also at a low level.

While paddy is the main food grain produced in the district groundnut and mulberry is the important commercial crop of the total area sown 27.0 per cent is under paddy and 39.8 per cent under groundnut. Further improvement in agricultural production in vellore is dependent on the use of improved and high yielding varieties of seeds extension of irrigation facilities for larger areas of land as also deployment of improved mechanical devices, besides bringing in fallow fold. Oil seeds sunflower cultivated in the district.

The rivers are not perennial and when they are in flood. Water are diverted into the channels through the anaicuts. The three important anicuts are the Palar, Cheyyar and Ponnai Anicuts. The palar anicut benefits the taluks of river Walajapet and Arakkonam, The anicut over Ponnai river benefits some lands in Arakkonam and Walajapet Taluks.

Animal Husbandary

Though no recognized superior breed of cattle is found in the district. The institute of Preventive Medicine at Ranipettai investigates on the diseases affiliating cattle goats and poultry and prepares serums to cure those diseases. According to the latest available figure there are six veterinary hospitals one veterinary dispensary cum key village centers 56 veterinary centers in the district. There is also a clinical laboratory and Animal

Diseases Intelligence Unit and 183 Veterinary Sub-centers in this districts.

Industries

The district has textile mills, sugar mills, fertilizerand insecticide factories etc. It is noted for its bidi manufacture and silk weaving. A continuous steel casting plan in the public sector has come up un Arakkonnam, The state Government has promoted an industrial complex in Ranipettai and a variety of products are manufactured in the units established in this industrial center. The largest number of factories in the district belong to the category Leather Tanning and curing. There are three sugar mills one each at vellore, Tirupattur and Ambur Silk Weaving is also popular and there are 32 factories engaging over 500 persons in this categort Valapandal and Walajapet are the important silk weaving centers in the district. Silk weaving is done as a household industry also. Weaving castes like vanniars, Naidus, Yadhavas, Gounders etc are said to be mostly engages in these jobs. Handlooms are important in Gudiyatham and certain other areas.

Sholinghur Block–Study Area

Sholinghur is one of the community Development block in Vellore district. Which is known for its hill temple Vallimalai Murugan and Kondapalayam murugan temple. It comes under walajapet taluk in vellore district.

Location and Area

Sholinghur block lies in the north side of the Vellore district, Sholinghur being the head town panchayat of this block and which is a small town in walajapet taluk of vellore district.

The block bounded on the north by Chittoor district of Andhra Pradesh on the east is Tiruttani Taluk of Chengalpet district, on the south by Arakkonam taluk of Velloe district and on the west by Gudiyatham Taluk of the same district.

According to the recent sources the total area of the block is 583 sq.km its total geographical area under land utilization is 70214 acres.

General Particulars

As per the recent data the total number of villages are 50 in this block. There are 45 Panchayats one town panchayat that is Sholinghur. The co operative socities are numbering 11 in this block.

Population

The total population of the blcok is 96,880 persons as per 1991 census. Of which 48670 male and 48210 female are constituted.

Table 4
Total Number of Population in Sholinghur Block as per 1991 Census

Section	*Population as per 1991 Census*
Male	48670
Female	48210
Total	96880

Source: 1991 Census Report.

The population in Sholinghur Town Panchayat alone is 21,412 persons, comprises 10781 males and 10631 females.

Table 5
Distribution of Villages of Population Ranges

Population Ranges	*Number of Villages*	*Percentage to column*
200-499	2	4.26
500-1999	25	53.18
2000-4999	18	38.30
5000-9999	2	4.26
Total	47	100

The details of percentage distribution of villages by population ranges as per 1991 census in Sholinghur block are given below in the table.

Table 6
Sholinghur Block

		Total	M	F
SC	Total Block	17695	8878	8817
	Town Population	1136	531	605
ST	Total Block	1003	483	520
	Town Population	234	113	121

As given in the Table 6 the total scheduled caste population in the Sholinghur Block is 17695 persons comprises 8878 male and 8817 female. The total scheduled Tribes population is 1136 persons comprises 531 male and 605 persons.

Sex Ratio

The sex ratio in sholinghur block as per 1991 census is the number of females per 1000 males 991 in this block and sec ration in this district is 1971.

Literacy Rate

The literacy rate in Sholinghur Block as per 1991 Census is 55.41 persons in which 71.17 per cent for male and 39.51 per cent for female. The details of literacy rate in sholimghur block and vellore district are given in the below table.

Table 7
Details of literacy Rate in Sholinghur Block

District Block	Male	Female	Total Persons
Sholinghur	71.17	39.51	54.41
Vellore	68.87	41.62	55.42

The percentage of main wokers in Sholinghur block as per 1991 census are 41.29 per cent, marginal workers are 2.94 Per cent and non-workers are 55.72 per cent. The details of percentage of main workers marginal workers and non-workers for rural population of Community Development block (Sholinghur Block) and Vellore District are presents in task below.

Table 8
Details of Worker in Sholinghur Block

Name	*Main Workers*			*Marginal/ Workers*			*Total Workers*			*Block/ District*		
	P	*M*	*F*	*P*	*M*	*F*	*P*	*M*	*F*	*P*	*M*	*F*
Sholinghur Blocl	41.29	55.97	26.28	2.94	0.73	5.17	44.28	56.70	31.65	55.77	43.30	68.35

The details of distribution of villages according to the availability of different amenities are presented below in the table.

The total area of the block as per the recent calculation (i.e. 1990-2000) is 583 Sq. km and the total geographical area in this block is 70214 acres. The area under cultivation is 33783 acres, The total forest covered in this Block is 430.4 acres. The permanent and incultivable land calculated to 9570.32 acres. The Permanent Pasture land is 738.68 acres. The total irrigated area is 9274 acresthe current fallow land in 8100 acres and the total wet and dry land are 14864.57 acres and 9274 acres respectively.

Soil Type

There are seven types of soil have been found the Sholinghur Block. These are Red Soil Which best and only one soil for cultivation of Mulberry other crops also can be cultivated in this soil. The area covered under this soil is 2613 acres, Red loan is 5817 acres, Craval soil 216 acres loan constitutes 3416 acres, clay is 277 acres, clay Loan 919 acres and alkaline is 47 acres. The major crops cultivated in this block are paddy, Sugarcane, Groundnut, Pulsus, Sunflower, Coconut, Ragi, Maize and other grains, The commercial crops are vegetables sericulture (i.e. Mulberry Cultivation).

Land Holdings

Small Farmers i.e one of two acres and below one access of land holder constituting 92 per cent in this block, marginal farmer i.e 2 to 4 acres of land holder constitutes 6 per cent and big farmers i.e above 4 acres land holders constitutes only 2 per cent in this block.

Irrigation Sources

The Rise Poinnai Flows through the Sholinghur block, which is being used for irrigation in this block, The other important irrigation sources are: Government Channels numbering 11, Public

Table 9
Details of Different Amenities

Name of the Block Dt	*No. of Disabled*	*Education Water*	*Medical T. Graph*	*Drinking Hat*	*Postal*	*Markert/*	*Communication*	*Approach by pucca*	*Power supply*
Sholinghur Block	47	46	23	47	59	9	39	33	47
		(97.87)	(48.94)	(100)	(61.70)	(19.15)	(88.98)	(70.21)	(100)
Vellore	808	760	328	808	519	123	692	635	808
		(94.06)	(40.59)	(100)	(64.23)	(15.22)	(85.64)	(78.59)	(100)

Source: Block Development Office, Sholinghur 1999.
Note: Figures in Brackets represent Percentages.
Utilisation of Land in Sholinghur Block .

Works Department (PWD) tanks are 37 and Municipals irrigation tanks 56 and wells including tube well numbering 8726 in this block.

The general particular in the Sholinghur Block the numver of Pattadar are 21127 numberof agricultural departments are numbering 2. The number of wells is 8726 the pumpsets numbered 3162 oil engines are 656 and the total tractors are 32 in this block.

Education

There are 82 Primary Schools, 14 middle schools, self financing primary and middle schools are 22 and scheduled castes and Tribes Primary are 6. The Government secondary schools are 5 in this district and there is one primary school for Backward Castes.

Notes and References

1. Action Plan Report of Deputy Director of Sericulture, Vellore, p. 115.
2. Hand Book of Agriculture, The Indian Council of Agriculture Research, New Delhi, 1997, p. 15.
3. Tamilnadu Administrative Report, 1988-89 to 1989-90, p. 131.
4. Bhatt S. C. (1995), *The Encyclopedia District Gazetteers of India.* Vol. II, Gyan Publishing House, New Delhi.
5. Report of Block Development of Office, Sholinghur, p. 25.
6. Action Plan Report of Technical Services Centre of Sericulture, Wallajapet, p. 99.

4

Socio-Economic Conditions of Sericulture Farmers

Sericulture is ont of the important components of Drought Prone Areas Programme in recent years. Under the programme a pilot project for mulberry cultivation under rainfed condition, in certain pockets of Vaniyambadi, Kaveripakkam, Walajapet taluks and under irrigated condition in other parts of the district and in the Block of Sholinghur in particular with a centrally sponsored Intensive Sericulture Development Programme and Special Integrated Rural Development Programme were important activities mto be mentioned.

This agro-based cottage industry is very labour intensive and employment generating, the important features of this industry is its high profitability, easy cultivation, quick returns and no labor problem these are all accelerates the agriculturist to cultivate more in the Vellore district and Sholinghur Block in particular.

Mulberry cultivation, silk worm rearing, silk reeling and finally silk weaving constitute the sequential order this major agro based industry which provides maximum employment opportunities and on the whole. The Sericulture programme is a good diversification activity to those engaged in agriculture. It is therefore becomes necessary to provide the basic infrastructure facilities for the rapid growth of this industry which has gained momentum during the recent years. The nature of assistance provided under the scheme was subsiding cost of cultivation of Mulberry, supply of rearing equipments at subsidized cost, creation of community Chowkies, creation of model farms. Sericulture developmental activity has to be further accelerated so that more and more people take up this as a complementary occupation to agriculture. The main objective of sericulture development will therefore continue to remain as one of providing a subsidiary occupation, besides agriculture in the district. The schemes under sericulture would therefore be one of creation of more infrastructure facilities rather than helping, the farmer with subsidy which is only temporary inn nature.

Sholinghur Block in Walajapet taluk of Vellore district is one of the major area cultivating Mulberry. There is a vast scope for this agro based industry, so an attempt has been made by the researcher towards the socio-economic conditions of sericulture farmers and the role of sericulture in improving the socio-economic status of the cultivators. This obviously requires an intensive study to understand and comment on the sericulture programme in "Sholinghur Block", the discussions towards this directions have been presented in this chapter.

The present study area Sholinghur Block having 320 mulberry cultivators at present? But only 25 per cent i.e., 80 samples have been selected for the study purpose in this block. The details of sample size are given in Table 1.

Table 1
Number of Respondents Cultivating Mulberry in Sholinghur Block (Sex Wise)

Group	*No. of Respondents*	*Total Mulberry Cultivator in the Sholinghur Block*
Male	54 (67.5)	230 (71.87)
Female	26 (32.5)	90 (28.13)
Total	80 (100)	320 (100)

As given in Table 1, the total sample size is 80 comprising 54 male cultivators (i.e., 67.5 per cents in the total sample size) and 26 female cultivators (i.e., 32.5 per cent in the total sample size). However, there are 320 mulberry cultivators in the Sholinghur Block in which Male and Female constitutes 71.87 per cent i.e., 230 persons and 28.14 per cent i.e., 90 persons respectively.

Details of community would be useful to know the socio-economic status of the respondents and also to criticize and suggest on government policies and schemes implemented, in any research work.

In this present study the researcher have been classified, the respondents into two categories only they are, the first one is scheduled Castes/Scheduled Tribes and the another one is other than SC/ST which includes all other communities. This is becauses only the SC/CT peoples are benefiting financial assistance from TAHDCO. The details are given in Table 2.

Table 2
Classifications of Community Among Samples in Sholinghur Block

Community	*No. of Respondents*	*Percentage*
SC/ST	23	28.75
Others	57	71.25

As given in Table 2, the Scheduled Castes and Scheduled Tribes constitutes 28.75 per cent in 23 farmers in the total respondents. The other communities such as Backwards Castes, Most Backwards and Forwards Castes constitutes remaing 71.28 per cent i.e., 57 farmers in the total 80 sample size.

It has been found that the Scheduled Castes and Tribes cultivators have been increasing because of they are getting subsidized financial assistance from TAHDCO and other agencies.

The educational status of the farmers in the sample size have been shown in Table 3.

Table 3

Educational Status	*No. of Respondents*	*Percentage*
Illiterate	21	26.25
Primary	11	13.75
Middle	36	45.00
S.S.L.C	6	7.5
Hr. Sec.	3	3.75
Graduate	2	2.5
Professional Technical	1	1.25
Total	80	100.00

As shown in Table 3 at the maximum of 45 present i.e., 36 farmers were studied Middle School i.e., 6th- 8th Illiterate were constituted 26.25 per cent i.e., 21 farmers next to middle next to middle schools. And it is noted that there is one professional/technical degree holder and two graduates among the sample size involving in this mulberry cultivation in Sholinghur Block. Other levels are contributes less proportions.

It has been observed through the sample size that any body can involve in this sericulture programme, even from illiterate to highly technical persons because sericulture department conducting training programmes about mulberry cultivation. So this becomes an easier to anybody.

There is always higher responsibilities for married persons in the family. And it is obvious from the sample size that have been taken for the purpose of knowing the martial status. The martial status of the respondents are indicated in Table 4.

Table 4
Marital Status of the Respondents

Particular	*No. of Respondents*	*Percentage*
Married	73	91.25
Unmarried	7	8.75

Sources: Primary.

As indicated in Table 4, in the total of 80 samples 91.25 per cent i.e., 73 of them are married in either sex male and female only 7 persons i.e., 8.75 per cent are unmarried in the total samples have been involved in mulberry cultivation activity. It has been observed by the Researcher that the female workers are doing an important and all major works in this activity.

The family members mainly childrens doing the major works of feeding, collecting cocoons and other workds. So there is necessary for children and family members for those family act involving in mulberry cultivation. The details of family members are given in Table 5.

Table 5
Details of Family Members Among the Respondents in Sholinghur Block

Classification	*Male*	*Female*	*Total*	*Average*
Child	88	60	148	74
	(38.94)	(29.55)	(34.50)	
Adult	138	143	218	14
	(61.06)	(70.44)	(65.50)	
Total	226	203	429	
	(100)	(100)	(100)	–

Sources: Primary.

As given in Table 5, the classification of family members are childs and adults in this study. The total male in the respondents family were 222 persons in which the composition of Childs and adults were 88 childs i.e., 38.94 per cent and 138 adults i.e., 61.06 per cent respectively. The total females are 203 persons, in which the respective shares of Childs and adults is 29.55 per cent i.e., 60 Childs and 70.44 per cent i.e., 143 adults.

The average of child in the total 80 family is 74 for both male and female. The adults are in the average of 141 for both male and female.

It is observed from the Table 5, that the adult female members are higher than the male members and the child female members are less compared to male child members. The inference could be that there is an opportunity for women's in self-employment generation through mulberry cultivation.

Occupational status is an important indicator of socio-economic status of a person. The occupational details of the sample size are given in Table 6.

Table 6
Occupational Status of the Respondents

Occupation	*No. of Respondents*	*Percentage*
Mulberry Cultivation	8	10.00
Agriculture and Mulberry Cultivators	67	83.75
Mulberry and Other Workers	5	6.25

Sources: Primary.

As given in Table 6, the occupations have been considered into three categories in this present study. They are 1. Mulberry cultivator; 2. Agriculture and mulberry cultivators; and 3. Mulberry and other workers.

In the total of 80 Samples more persons about 67 Persons i.e 83.75 per cent are involving in the activities of agriculture with sericulture. The Persons who are cultivating mulberry alone are 8 Persons, which is 10 Per cent in total samples. And finally 6.25 per cent of the respondents are doing mulberry and other works. The other work is daily wage.

It has been found that most of the cultivators are doing both agriculture and sericulture in the total of 326 mulberry cultivators in the Sholinghur block. The only Mulberry Cultivating persons are should be increased inorder to step up the mulberry cultivation in this block and the district as a whole.

The details of land holding in the sample size are presented in Table 7.

As shown in Table 7 the land holdings have been classified into three catrogories they are (1) Marginal Farmers Having land holding upto two acres (2) small farmers having land holding from 2 to 5 acres; and (3) big farmers having land holding above five acres.

The marginal farmers constitutes 78.95 per cent in the total samples of 80, i.e 63 farmers are marginal farmers only two farmers i.e. 2.5 per cent in the total sample are having land holding above five acres. The remaining 18.75 per cent i.e 15 farmers belongs to small farmers.

Table 7
Details of Land Holding in the Sample Size

Items	*No. of Respondents*	*Land in acres*	*Average Land Holding (Acres)*
Mariginal Farmers (upto 2 AC)	63	112.95	1.79
	(78.75)	(62.21)	
Small Farmers (2-5 AC)	15	56.60	3.77
	(18.75)	(31.18)	
Big Farmers (Aboe 5 AC)	2	12.00	6.00
	(2.5)	(6.61)	
Total	80	181.55	2.27
	(100)	(100)	

Source: Primary.
Note: Figure in Brackets represent percentage.

The total land holding of the 80 sample farmers is 181.55 acres of which the respective shares of marginal farmers small farmers and big farmers is 62.21 per cent i.e 112.95 acres; 31.18 per cent i.e 56.60 acres; and 6.61 per cent i.e 12 acres in the Sholinghur Block.

The average land holding of the three mentioned categories are 1.79 acres, 3.77 acres and 6 acres respectively.

It has been found that there is a higher share of marginal farmers at an average land holding of 1.79 acres in Sholinghur Block. And this is obvious that the size of land holding is reducing due to the population explosions.

The details of Cultivating patter in Sholinghur Block are shown in Table 8.

Table 8
Pattern of Cultivation and Land Utilisation in Sholinghur Block

Utilisation of land	*Land in Use Acre*	*Percentage*
Mulberry Cultivation	57.40	31.62
Agriculture	100.15	55.16
Waste Land	24.00	13.22
Total Land	181.55	100.00
Total Land Under Cultivation	157.55	86.78

Source: Primary.

As shown in Table 8 the total land holding of the sample size is 181.55 acres. But the total land under culvitation is 157.55 acres i.e 86.78 per cent of land only under utilization of which the per centage of utilization for agriculture is higher i.e 56.26 per cent. The utilization of mulberry cultivation constitutes 31.61 per cent and the share of waste land is 13.22 per cent which considerably higher.

It is observed that the propotion of waste land is considerably higher in the Sholinghur Block. To Reduce the waste land the cultivation of mulberry and agriculture should be motivated through beneficial programmes.

Housing is one of the basic necessity of the human beings. It is said to be that food, cloth and shelter is the basic necessities of human beings without which a man considered to be below poverty. So housing is the one component, which ultimately reflects the socio- economic status of a person. The details of housing status of the sample size in Sholinghur Block have been shown in Table 9.

Table 9
Housing Status of the Sample Size.

Type of House	*No.of Respondents*	*Percentage*
Pucca	28	35.00
Semi pucca	11	13.75
Kutcha	6	7.50
Thatched	35	43.75
Total	80	100.00

Source: Primary.

As given in Table 9 The status of housing has been classified into Pucca, Semi - Pucca, Kutcha and Thatched. In the total of 80 Samples 35 Persons i.e 43.75 per cent have owned Thatched houses and next to this 28 persons i.e 35 per cent are owning Pucca houses. The other two of Semi pucca and Kutcha are 13.75 per cent and 7.50 per cent Respectively.

It has been found that the number of Pucca houses have been increased in this Sholinghur Block because of Housing is a compulsory one of the developmental programme implemented by TAHDCO and other agencies.

And also it has been found out that the every beneficiary of TAHDCO and other agencies getting a pucca house.

In conclusion the Government agencies should give financial assistance to houseless the thatched house owning people inorder to step up the housing status of the cultivator.

The cultivators getting financial assistance from various agencies to construct houses. The details of sources of finances in selected sample size in Sholinghur Block of Walajapet taluk are indicated in Table 10.

Table 10
Sources of Financial Assistance for Construction of Houses

Source	*No. of Respondents*	*Percentage*
Own Funds	64	80.00
TAHDCO	15	18.75
DRDA Group House	1	1.25
Total	80	100.00

Source: Primary.

As Indicated in Table 10 the sources of finances for construction of houses are consists own funds. TAHDCO and DRDA group House scheme. 80 Per cent of the total 80 Respondents i.e. 64 Person constructed the house on their own funds. 18.75 Per cent i.e. 15 Persons had constructed their house by TAHDCO assistance, And only 1.25 per cent i.e. Only one person among the respondents have been got financial assistance from DRDA Group House Scheme.

It has been revealed that from the Sample Size, Government agencies have been playing a small role in the improvement of housing status of the mulberry cultivators in the Sholinghur Block in Particular and the whole district in general.

The details of total family expenditure of sample respondents, they are food and clothe, education, festival and recreation are shown in Table 11.

Table 11
Total Family Expenditure of Respondents
(Food and Cloth Education Festival and Recreation)

Size of Expenditure	*No. of Respondents*	*Percentage*
5001-7000	42	52.50
7001-9000	33	41.25
9001-11000	7	8.75
11001 and above	11	13.75
Total	80	100.00

Source: Primary.

As shown in Table 11 The total family expenditure of total respondents have been taken in the following manner. (1) Persons spending upto Rs. 7000 are 42 Persons i.e. 52.50 per cent (2) Persons spending 7001 to Rs. 9000 are 33 persons i.e 41.25 per cent 3) person spending Rs. 9001 to 11,000 are 7 Persons i.e 8.75 per cent and 4) 11001 and above are numbering 11 Persons i.e. 13.75 per cent .

It has been found that 52.50 per cent of the peoples spending rupees for their expenditure upto Rs. 7000. And also observed that people spending money more than 10,000 for their family expenditure have been very less. It is obvious from the above discussions that the economic status of the farmers yet to be improve in this Sholinghur Block and in the district as well.

The details of income structure of the Mulberry Cultivators in Sholinghur Block is Shown in Table 12.

Table 12
Income of the Respondents

Income Structure	*No. of Respondents*	*Percentage*
5000-10000	27	33.75
10001-15000	33	41.25
15001-20000	10	12.5
20001-25000	4	5.00
25001 and above	6	7.50

Source: Primary.

As shown in Table 12 the income structure of mulberry cultivator have been categorized in the following manner. (1) the persons getting income upto Rs. 10000 per annum are 27 i.e 33.75 per cent (2) persons getting income from Rs. 10001 to Rs. 15000 is 33 Persons i.e. 41.25 Persons (3) persons getting annual income from s. 15001 to 20000 is 10 Persons i.e. 12.5 Per cent. (4) persons getting annual income from Rs. 20001 to Rs. 25000 is 4 i.e., 5 Per cent and (5) those who are getting annual income above 25000 are 6 in the total sample respondents in Sholinghur Block.

It is found that the cultivators in the Sholinghur Block getting annual income at an average of rupees 5000 to 15000. Only few are getting their annual income above Rs. 20000.

In Conclusion the cultivators should be induced more to cultivate the commercial crops like sericulture.

Savings indicated the improvement of economic status of a person or in the economy as a whole. The details of savings among the respondents in Sholinghur Block is presented in Table 13.

Table 13
Savings Details of Respondents in Sholinghur Block

Institutions	*No. of Respondents*	*Percentage*
Own Funds	11	13.75
Insurance	5	6.25
Chits & Funds	1	1.25
Commercial Banks	7	8.75
Assests	7	8.75
Jewels	17	21.25
Saving Less	32	40.00
Total	32	100.00

Source: Primary.

As presented in Table 13 the sources of savings are Post Office, Insurance, Chits & Funds, Commercial Banks, Assest in Hand and in the form of Jewells.

As per the sample survey 40 per cent of the people are savingless i.e 32 cultivators out of 80 samples. However in the saving side peoples are mostly like to save their money in the form of jewels. Another source of saving that people like to save their money in Post Office. 13.75 per cent of the respondents having savings in Post office. Insurance and Commercial banks did not make much impression in rural people to save their money. However it is obvious that the rural people don't have resources to save and they are in the position "Hand To Mounth".

It has been found that the savingless are constitutes major proportions in the rural areas, this is because of they don't have excess income to save, even sometimes their expenditure exceeds their income. So it is necessary for the government to implement an effective "Action Plans" to improve their agricultural and allied income for better saving.

And another one is that Commercial banks should play a vital role in increasing the saving habit among the rural peoples.

Credit Facilities of Sericulture

The co-operative Banks, Commercial Banks and TAHDCO are serving as purveyors of credit in the rural areas, These three financial institutions playing a vital role in developing the sericulture programme. It is important to noet here that these three institutions are in a ready position to grant credit facilities on the basis of different sericulture programmes that were to be implemented by Sericultural Department. Apart from this the Credits has to be provided by Commercial Banks can be refinanced by NABARD.

Bank Loans for the Following Activities

1. Loans for Plantation of Mulberry
2. Loans for Purchasing of raw materials
3. Loans for Construction of rearing sheds,'
4. Loans for increasing the irrigational facilities
5. Loans for construction of silk reeling centers.

The above all loan provided in the form of short term loans and medium term loans, The first four types of loans can be considered as agricultural loan and the fifth one can be taken as Industrial Loan.

Eligibility for Getting Loan from Banks

The beneficiary Should satisfy the following criteria for getting loans from the Co-operatives and commercial Banks.

1. He should cultivate mulberry atleast in 0.50 acres in his own land.
2. He should belongs with in the service area of the Particular Bank in which he is approaching.
3. He Should not have due in any other bank.
4. Should be cultivate in a particular survey number and particular area.

Details of Loan Amount

The details of loan amount on the basis of NABARD letter dated on 13.05.1993 are shown in the Table 14.

Table 14

Particulars	*One acre*	*0.50 Acre*
Crop Loan	2715	700
Rearing Shed	15000	10000
Raw materials	2750	2250
Laying and wage etc	3180	-
Total	23645	12980

As given in the Table 14 the loan for rearing shed is Rs. 15000 for one acre irrigated area. I.e. 260-300 sq. feet. And Rs. 10000 for 0.50 cultivated area i.e. about 200 sq. feet.

Rate of Interest

The rate of interest that has been imposed and collected by banks is 11.5 Per cent upto Rs. 7500 and from 7500 to 25000 the interest rate is 13.5 per cent. The loan amount increased to 33600 for one acre at present. The rate of interest is 13% and 15% at present.

Patter of Loan

The loan sanctioning pattern is divided into three instalments (1) the First instalment is consisting crop loans. And only for construction of base level for rearing shed. (2) in the second instalement is for finishing of rearing shed (3) in the third installment finishing of construction works of shed and purchasing of raw materials. The loans can be repayable two times in a year.

The sources of debt for sericulture in the Sholinghur Block is Indicated in Table 15.

Table 15
Sources of Debts in the Sample Size

Sources	*No. of Respondents*	*Percentage*
Friends and Relative	13	16.25
Money Lenders	12	15.00
Co-operative Society	14	17.50
Commercial Banks	10	12.50
TAHDCS	15	18.75
Debt Less	16	20.00
Total	80	100.00

Source: Primary.

As indicated in Table 15 the sources for debt in sericultural programme are following (1) Friends and Relatives Constitutes 16.25 Per cent i.e 13 Persons among the total of 80 Respondents (2) Monet Lender contributes 15 per cent (3) Co-operatives Shares 17.50 per cent (4) 12.50 per cent Shared by Commercial Bank and Maximum of 18 per cent in the total sample is contributed by TAHDCO. However the debtless are constitutes considerable proportion i.e. 20 per cent.

It has been found that the most of the sericulture farmers depends largely on debt and the all financial institution and non-financial institutions Shares more or less equal contributions. And also it has been observed that the cultivators cultivating mulberry mainly for the purpose of getting financial assistance.

As indicated in the Table 16 The awareness of sericultural programmes that were implemented by TAHDCO among the respondents is only 18.75 per cent i.e only 15 Persons in the total 80 Samples.However 81.25 per cent of the cultivators are unware of the TAGDCO implemented sericulture programmes.

Table 16
Awareness of Sericulture Programme Implemented by TAHDCO among Respondent

Particulars	*No. of Respondents*	*Percentage*
Awared	15	18.75
Un-Awared	65	81.25
Total	80	100.00

It is revealed that the TAHDCO implemented sericulture programme is not much effective among cultivators. So the Programme should be implemented in more effective manner.

It has been observed from the Table 17. That the Mulberry cultivators came to know about the sericultural programmes largely by meeting camp and Training Programmes this constitutes the large Proportions of 63.75 per cent. 25 per cent of the cultivators came to know through Department staff.

Table 17

Sources	*No. of Respondents*	*Percentage*
Audio & Video	1	1.25
Phamplets	1	1.25
Camp	51	63.75
Exhibition	7	8.75
Department Staff	20	25.00
Total	80	100.00

The inference could be that there should be an effective organizing meeting and camp in the District Level. Block Level and Village Level. And another one is that there should be a attractive incentive schemes for staff to lift up the training Programmes for more mulberry cultivation in this Block and District as well.

The opinions of respondents on the income from sericulture has been observed by The "Researcher" Maximum of 71.25 Per cent of the respondents were of the opinion that the income from sericulture is lower than that of agriculture. Only 28.75 per cent of the respondents were of the opinion that the income from sericulture is higher than agriculture. The details are given in Table 18.

It is Proved that the sericulture programme is one of the agro-based cottage industry playing major role next to agriculture in developing the rural economy.

Table 18
The Opinion of Respondents on the Income from Sericulture and Agriculture

Particulars	*No. of Respondents*	*Percentage*
High Income	23	28.75
Low Income	57	71.25
Total	80	100.00

Source: Primary.

The details of Mulberry Production in Vellore District is given in Table 19.

Table 19
Details of Mulberry Production in Vellore District From 1995-96 to 1998-99

Year	*Mulberry Plantation in acre*	*Egg Hatching*	*Produced Cocoonin Kg*
1995-96	132.45	305000	1024000
1996-97	192.40	132182	74598
	(45.26)	(-56.66)	(92.72)
1997-98	104.75	133846	51254
	(-45.56)	(1.26)	(-31.29)
1998-99	99.75	174000	43000
	(-4.77)	(30.00)	(-16.10)
Total	529.35	745028	1192852

Source: Report of the Joint Director of Sericulture Office, Vellore 1999.
Note: Figures in Brackets Represent Annual Growth Rate.

As given Table 19 The mulberry Plantation in Vellore District was 132.45 acres in 1995 - 96 and the same was increased to 192.40 in 1996-97. Then the following years it has been reducing. The growth rate of mulberry plantation has been showing a negative. Trend in the following two subsequent years i.e. 1997-98 and 1998-99. mt. 7.

The cocoon production also showing a negative trend in vellore district from 1995-96 to 1998-99.

The study revealed that the sericulture programmes in the Vellore district is in the deteriorating stage. So suitable measures should be taken by the Government to rectify them.

The details of total loan amount sanctioned by Financial institutions to cultivators are shown in Table 20.

Table 20
Total Loan Sanctioned by Financial Institutions to the Total Respondents

Particulars	*Amount in Rupees*
Net Loan Amount	4,57,900
Subsidiary	2,65,000
Total Loan Amount	7,22,900
Amount Repaid	4,57,900
No. of Installment	5 Years
Rate of Interest	15%

Source: Primary.

The important reason for the success of 100 per cent repayment in the loan amount, which has been found by the researcher is that the financial institution sanctioning the loan amount after taking repayment amount except subsidy, That is the borrowers repaying the loan amount at the time of borrowal. Ultimately non-repayment problem is not arising in the mulberry cultivation.

The details of expenditure on Sericultural activities are presented in Table 21.

Table 21
Details of Expenditure on Sericulture Activity in the Blcok

Particulars	*1 Acre Unit*	*½ Unit*
Mulberry Cultivation Expenses		
Planting Material	1650.00	825.00
Farm Yard Manure	500.00	250.00
Fertilizers	490.00	245.00
Perticides	75.00	40.00
Labour Cost	2080.00	1040.00
	4795.00	2400.00

Contd...

Particulars	1 Acre Unit	½ Unit
Rearing Equipments		
Trays	800.00	400.00
Montages	1200.00	600.00
Wooden Stands	750.00	375.00
Chemical & Nets	500.00	250.00
Layings	600.00	300.00
	3850.00	1925.00
	15000.00	10000.00
Rearing Shed Only		
Total Expendes	23645.00	14325.00
	(or)	(or)
	23600.00	14300.00

Source: Action Plan Report 1998-99, Technical Services Centre, Walajapet.

The total expenses of Sericultural activities for 0.50 Acre amounting to Rs. 14300 to 14325.

The details of income from sericulture is given in Table 22.

Table 22

Particulars	1 Acre Unit (rs)
First Year	
Layings	400
Cocoon Production	149Kg
Cocoon Price for kg Rs 80	140 x 80
Total Income	11,200.00
Net Profit	9,120,00
Second Year	
1000 Layinsg	1000
Cocoons production	350 Kg
Perkg to Cocoon Price Rs. 80	350 x 80
Total Income	28,000.00
Expenses	4,000.00
Net Profit	24,000.00

The researcher have been observed while asking the respondents opinion about their satisfication in mulberry cultivation. The details are given in Table 23.

Table 23
Satisfication of Mulberry Cultivators in Mulberry Cultivation among Respondents

Items	*No. of Respondents*	*Percentage*
Satisfication	67	83.75
Unsatisfication	13	16.25
Total	80	100.00

Source: Primary.

Only 16.25 per cent were of the opinion that they are unsatisfied the study reveals that the sericultural programme has sector generating more employment especially for women and childrens and it is one industry whose operations are easy in the Sholinghur Block at Vellore district. However effective Policy Measures and more financial assistance could be provided in the Sholinghur Block to the success of this programme.

Many Problems have been observed by the "Researcher", While Investigating the Mulberry Cutivators.

Problems of Sericulture Development

Any Planned development of sericulture has to programme for a higher growth rate than the normal.

The mulberry farmer who is usually a small farmer constitutes the backbone for the sustained spreads of sericulture. Unless his problems are identified for taking necessary remedial action, planned programme of development may not be successful targeted growth cannot be achieved. Hence an attempt is made by the researcher to identify the problems of the sericulturist in order to focus the factors which operate as constraints in the development on sericulture which is now bristling with problem of technology, marketing, finance, extension and organization.

Scarcity of Seed

The marked inadequacy of the existing infrastructure of grain ages, the basic seed farms and seed areas for the production of both local race and foreign seed cocoons and its under utilization account for the absence of self-sufficiency in the supply of the seed. The existing arrangements for seed multiplication for seed multiplication and distribution are not in proportion to the area under mulberry cultivation.

Marketing

Seri-culturists in Vellore in particular and Tamilnadu in general are experiencing a great difficulty in marketing their cocoons. All the sericulturist in the course of survey emphasized the need for regulated markets under the Government organization. Absence of proper marketing facilities constitutes the prime obstacle for the orderly and rapid development of sericulture in the district.

Minimum Price and Price Fluctuations

No Steady growth of an industry is possible without stable and minimum economic price for its products and sericulture and silk industries are no exception. There are violent fluctuations in sericulture industry for a number of reasons. Instability of cocoon crops. Wide variations in the quality of cocoons harvested absence of standarisation and quality control, Poor Marketing facilities are responsible for wide fluctuations in the prices of Cocoons. During Rainy season the quality of cocoon is poorer, yield is somewhat higher, the supply in the market is greater, leading to fall in the price.

Reeling Industry

A significant week link in the development of sericulture in the state in general and vellore in particyular is the inadequate growth of reeling industry.

An efficient reeling industry is essential to afford market for cocoons on the one hand and the supply of raw material, raw silk for the manufacturing industry on the other. Production of more cocoons without arrangement for reeling would bring down the prices of cocoons thereby undermining income of the sericulturists and employment for the local people.

Credit Facilities

The two complaints of the sericulturists as regards the institutional finance are delay and some corruption.

The main complaints of the sericulturist that the institutional financial agencies are too conservative to extend crop loans to sericulturist. If they can get crop loans, the problem of financial resources for sericulturist. If they can get crop loans, the problems of financial resources for sericulturists can be solved to a great extent and the area needs proper assessments and encouragement of the farmers.

The credit supplied by the institutional agencies is meager and inadequate. The commercial banks which have to play a significant role are not evincing any interest. Even a lead bank are not forthcoming to finance sericulture activity. For an orderly development of sericulture the institutional agencies should identify the special features and needs of sericulture and the magnitude of finance required for fixed and working capital and extend support under an integrated approach in view of the economic importance of sericulture, Development of sericulture under any perspective planning becomes a difficult job.

Availability of adequate extension staff is one requirement and their dedicated service is another requistie in any case speedy gowth of sericulture involving innovation on the part of farmers will not be feasible without the establishment of a competent extension service department which has to enlighten the farmers, give advice and augument the entrepreneurial abilities of the small farmers give advice and augment the entrepreneutial abilities of the small farmers. So the sericulture department has to buid up competent extension cadre,

Drudgery in Silk Work Rearing

Although mulberry gardening required better knowledge and skills to handle the cultivation as compared to several crop enterprises, The one activity which will be quite strange to the normal farmer is the silkworm rearing which may be a completely new activity if he had no opportunity to be familiar with it. Silkworm rearing needs careful handling, patience and perseverance to look after their growth. Most of the farmers feel that feeding silkworm in the late hours of the night involves drudgery and makes the farming families tired. Hence the drudgery constitutes one of the obstacles for speedy growth of sericulture.

Climatic Hazard

Cool and equable climate throughout the year is quite conducive for silkworm rearing, cocoon production and high Renditta. Climatic extremes upset the realization of sericulture productivity. It has been pointed out that in the hot tropical climate. Especially during summer new techniques like the use of air cooler, dripping of water on the rearing sheds, arranging the rearing rooms under the shade of big trees are adopted to facilitate cocoon production. These techniques increase the cost of production marginally, but the hot climate adversely affects the quality and yield of cocoons, thereby reducing the income per acre under sericulture. High Leaf yield from mulberry garden located in good soil with irrigation facilities many compensate for the higher cost arising out the extreme summer climate. In any case the climatic hazard adds to the drudgery of silk worm rearing involving greater care and attention on the part of sericulturists increasing their managerial responsibility requiring more time.

Hence, other thing being equal, hot climate is a deterrent for sericulture entrepreneurship. As sericulture is a labour-intensive enterprise, high wages that prevail in the agricultural growth centers also constitute an obstacle for sericultural expansion. Big farmers while they process better capacity to face the climatic hazards, may not like the increased managerial responsibility and time required to look after the sericulture. Small farmers lack resources to provide adequate facilities to counteract the hazard of summer heat of silkworm rearing. These aspects are to be considered in spreading sericulture to new areas.

5

Summary and Conclusion

Sericulture is one of the important components of Drought Prone areas programme in Vellore District, Particularly in Sholinghur Block of Walajapet taluk in recent Years.

This agro-based cottage industry is very labour intensive and employment generating the important features of this industry is its high profitability, easy cultivation, quick returns and no labour problem these all accelerates the agriculturist to cultivate more in the Vellore District and Sholinghur Block in Particular.

Mulberry Cultivation, Silk worm rearing, silk reeling and finally silk weaving constitute the sequential order this major agro-based industry which provides maximum employment opportunities and on the whole. The sericulture programme is a good diversification activity to those engages in agriculture. It is therefore becomes necessary to provide the basic infrastructural facilities for the rapid growth of this industry which has gained momentum during the recent years. The nature of assistance provided under the scheme was subsidizing cost of cultivation of mulberry supply of rearing equipments at subsidisided cost, creation of community chowkies, creation and model farms. Sericulture developmental activity has to be further accelerated so that more and more people take up this as a complementary occupation to agriculture. The main objective of sericulture development will therefore continue to remain as one of providing a subsidiary occupation, besides agriculture in the district. The schemes under sericulture would therefore to be one of creation of more infrastructure facilities rather than helping the farmer with subsidy which is only temporary in nature.

Sholinghur Block in Walajapet taluk of Vellore District is one of the major area cultivating mulberry. There is a vast scope for the agro-based industry. So an attempt has been made by the researcher towards the socio-economic conditions of sericulture farmers and the role of sericulture in improving the socio-economic status of the cultivators.

Objectives

1. To assess the socio-economic conditions of the sericulture farmers in Sholinghur Block, Vellore District,
2. To evaluate the sustainable role of TAHDCO in sericulture farming in the study area.
3. To findout the problems and prospects in Sericulture.

Methodology

The research design of the study was empirical and descriptive. The study mainly based on Primary data. SO samples out of 320 total sericulture farmers were selected at random in 10 villages of Sholinghur Block in Vellore District. The necessary data were collected by making use of elaborate and well prepared questionnaire. May 1999, June 1999 and August 1999 has been spent for collecting data. The collected data was consolidated, tabulised and interpreted carefully. The analysis was carried on by applying simple statistical tools like percentages, average and growth rate, pictoral representation were also made use of in its study.

Findings

1. There are 320 Mulberry cultivator in the Sholinghur Block in which Male and Female constitutes 71.87 per cent i.e., 230 persons and 28.13 per cent i.e 90 Persons respectively.
2. The Scheduled castes and Scheduled Tribes Constitutes 28.75 per cent in 23 farmers in the total respondents. The other communities such as Backward castes, Most Backward and Forward Castes constitutes remaining 71.28 per cent i.e. 57 farmers in the total 80 Sample Size.

   It has been found that Scheduled Castes and Tribes Cultivators have been increasing because of they are getting subsidized financial assistance from TAHDCO and other agencies.
3. It has been observed through the sample size that any body can involve in this sericulture programme, even from illiterate to highly technical persons because sericulture department conducting training programe about mulberry cultivation. SO this become an easier to anybody.
4. It has been observed by the Researcher that the female workers are doing an important and all major works in this activity
5. The average of childs in the total 80 family is 74 for both male and female. The adults are in the average of 141 for both male and female.

   It is observed from the Table 4.5 that the adult female members are higher than the male member and the child female members are less compared to male child members. The inference could be that there is an opportunity for women's in self employment generation through mulberry cultivation.
6. In the total of 80 Samples more persons about 67 Persons i.e. 83.75 per cent are involving in the activities of agriculture with sericulture. The persons who are cultivating mulberry alone are 8 persons which is 10 per cent in total samples. And

finally 6.25 per cent of the respondents are doing mulberry and other works. The other work is daily wage.

7. The marginal farmers constitutes 78.95 per cent in the total sample of 80 i.e. 63 farmers are marginal farmers only two farmers. I.e 2.5 per cent in the total sample are having land holding above five acres. The remaining 18.75 per cents i.e 15 farmers belongs to small farmers.

   The average land holding of the three mentioned categories are 1.79 acres 3.77 acres and 6 acres respectively.

   It has been found that there is a higher share of marginal farmers at an average land holding of 1.79 acres in Sholinghur Block, and this is obvious that the size of land holding is reducing due to the population explosion.

8. The total land holding of the sample size is 181.55 acres. But the total land under cultivation is 157.55 acres. I.e. 86.78 per cent of land only under utilization of which the per centage of utilisation for mulberry cultivation constitutes 31.61 per cent and the share of waste land is 13.22 Per cent which considerably higher.

9. In the total of 80 samples 35 persons i.e 43.75 have owned thatched houses and next to this 28 Persons. I.e. 35 Per cent are owning pucca houses. The other two of semi pucca and Kutcha are 13.75 per cent and 7.50 per cent respectively.

   It has been found that that number of pucca houses have been increased in this Sholinghur Block Because of housing is a compulsory one in the developmental programme implemented by TAHDCO and other agencies.

10. Eighty per cent of the total 80 respondents i.e. 64 persons constructed the house on their own funds. 18.75 per cent i.e. 15 persons had constructed their house by TAHDCO assistance. And only 1.25 per cent i.e. only one person among the respondents have been got financial assistance from DRDA Group House Scheme.

It has been revealed that from the sample size. Governernment agencies have been playing a small role in the improvement of Housing status of the mulberry cultivators in the Sholinghur Block in particular and the whole district in general.

11. The total family expenditure of total respondents have been taken in the following manner. (1) Persons spending upto Rs. 7000 are 42 persons i.e 52.50 per cent. (2) Persons spending 7001 to Rs. 9000 are 33 Persons i.e.e 41.25 per cent (3) Persons spending Rs. 9001 to 11,000 are 7 Persons i.e. 8.75 per cent and (4) 11001 and above are numbering 11 Persons i.e. 13.75 per cent.
12. The income structure of mulberry cultivator have been categorized in the following manner (1) the persons getting income upto Rs.10000 per annum are 27 i.e 33.75 per cent (2) Persons getting income from Rs. 10001 to Rs. 15000 is 33 persons i.e. 41.25 persons (3) persons getting annual income from Rs.15001 to 20000 is 10 persons I,e. 12.5 per cent (4) persons getting annual income from Rs. 20001 to Rs. 25000 is 4 i.e 5 per cent and (5) those who are getting annual income above 25000 are 6 in the total samples respondents in Sholinghur Block.
13. It is found that the cultivators in the Sholinghur Block getting annual income at an average of rupees 5000 to 150000. Only few are getting their annual income above Rs. 20000.
14. Peoples are mostly like to save their money in the form of jewels. Another source of saving that people like to save their money is post office. 13.75 per cent of the respondents having savings in post Office. Insurance and Commercial Banks did not make much impression in rural people to save their money.
15. It has been found that the most of the sericultural farmers depends largely on debt and the all financial institutions and non-financial institutions shares more or less equal contributions. And also it has been observed that the

cultivators cultivating mulberry mainly for the purpose of getting financial assistance.

16. It has been observed from the Table 17. That the mulberry cultivators came to know about the sericultural programmes largely by meeting camp and Training Programmes. This constitutes the large proportions of 63.75 per cent. 25 per cent of the cultivators came to know through Department Staff.
17. Maximum of 71.25 per cent of the respondents were of the opinion that the income from sericulture is lower than that of agriculture. Only 28.75 per cent of the respondents were of the opinion that the income from sericulture is higher than agriculture.
18. The mulberry plantation in vellore District was 132.45 acres ub 1995-96 and the same was increased to 192.40 in 1996-97 Then the following years it has been reducing. The growth rate of mulberry plantation has been showing a negative trend in the following two subsequent years. I.e. 1997-98 and 1998 -99.
19. The important reason for the success of 100 per cent repayment in the loan amount, which has been found by the researcher is that the financial institution sanctioning the loan amount after taking repayment amount except subsidy. That is the borrowers repaying the loan amount at the time of borrower. Ultimately non-repayment problem is not rising in the Mulberry cultivation.
20. It has been found that the income from second year of cultivation is higher than that of the first year. It sis doubled of the first year amount. The obvious reason for the more income in the second year is absence of infrastructure cost.

Suggestions

1. It has been found that most of the cultivators are doing both agriculture and sericulture in the total of 320 mulberry

cultivators in the Sholinghur Block. The only mulberry cultivating persons are should be increased inorder to step up the mulberry cultivation in this block and the district as a whole.

2. It is observed that the proportion of waste land is considerably higher in the Sholinghur Block. To Reduce the waste land the cultivation of mulberry and agriculture should be motivated through beneficial programmes.

3. It has been found out that the every beneficiary of TAHDCO and other agencies getting a pucca house.

   In conclusion the government agencies should give financial assistance to houseless and thatched house owning people inorder to step up the housing status of the cultivator.

4. It has been found that 52.5 per cent of the peoples spending rupees for their expenditure upto Rs.7000. And also observed that people spending money more than 10000 for their family expenditure have been very less. It is obvious from the above discussions that the economic status of the farmers yet to be improve in this Sholinghur Block and in the district as well.

5. The cultivators should be induced more to cultivate the commercial crops like sericulture.

6. It has been found that the savingless are constitutes major proportions in the rural areas. This is because of they don't have excess income to save even sometimes their expenditure exceeds their income. So it is necessary for the government to implement an effective "Action Plans" to improve their agricultural and allied income for better saving and another one is that Commercial Banks should play a vital role in increasing the saving habit among the rural peoples.

7. There Should be an effective organizing meeting and camp in the District level. Block Level and Village Level. And another one is that there should be a attractive incentive schemes for staff to lift up the training programmes for more mulberry cultivation in this Block and District as well.

8. The study revealed that the Sericulture Programmes in the Vellore District is in the deteriorating stage. So suitable measures should be taken by the Government to rectify them.
9. Their should be a fixed rate of cocoon in the market.
10. There is a need for crop failure insurance.
11. The import of raw silk must be stoped for better future for Indian silk.

Conclusion

Sericulture being one of the main agro-based cottage industry, has the growth potentially in Vellore District especially in Sholinghur Block, the development of Sericulture in this Block is a progressive one compare to other Blocks in the Vellore District. More credit facilities and effective training and meetings camps would increase the sericulture farming. Sericulture therefore, deserces encouragement not only to produce silk but also to generate employment opportunities in rural India. It is obvious from the foregoing study that sericulture would play a pivotal role in shapping the economic destiny of the downtrodden, by providing lucrative income and employment.

Bibliography

Books

Balasubramanian a devsloping and azotobacter biofertilizer for mulberry,department of agri microbiology and regional research station, Paiyar, Tamilnadu agricultural University, Coimbatore. 1995

Bhatt S. C. (1971), The Encyclopedic District Gazetteers of India, Volume-2, Gyan Publishing House, New Delhi.

F.A.O., Manual on Sericulture-I Mulberry Cultiavtion Rome.

Grish Shani, Kamte I. A, Sericulture Development in Non-Traditional Areas, BAIF, Development Research Foundation, Pune, India.

Hand Book of Agriculture. The Indian Council of Agriculture Research, New Delhi, 1997.

Handlooms Census of 1973.

Hanumpappa M. G., Sericulture of Rural Development, Himalaya Publishing House, New Delhi.

Koshy T. D. (1993), Silk Exports and Development, Ashish Publishing House, New Delhi.

Narasimhan M. Hand book of Practical Sericulture, Central Silk Board.

Perumalswamy S. S., Economic Development of Tamilnadu, Chand & Company Limited, New Delhi.

Ramana D. V., Economics of Sericulture and Silk Industry in India, Deep & Deep Publication, New Delhi.

Times of India, Year Book, 1971.

Journals/Articles

Down to Earth, March 15, 1999.

Indian Farming, July, 1997.

Industrial Herald, December, 1998.

Indian Journal of Sericulture, Published by the Central Silk Board, 1991, 1994, 1998.

Indian Silk, Central Silk Board, Banglore.

Khadigramodyog, February, 1997.

Kurukshetra, June 1995, June 1998.

Monthly *Abstract of Statistics*

Tamil Nadu Administration Report, 1998 - 99, 1989-90

Tikk M. K. (1999), Tangled Threads Silk Growers and Imports, *Economic and Political Weekly*, March 6-13.

Social Welfare, June 1995

Sunday, 11-17 April, 1999

Unpublished Thesis

Sericulture Available Agro Industrial Occupation A. Focus on Progressive Sericulture District of Tamilnadu, M.Phil, Dissertation Submitted by Balasubramaniyam. S. University of Madras, 1984.

Abbreviations

CB	-	Cross Breed
CSB	-	Central Silk Board
DFLs	-	Disease Free Layings
DRDA	-	District Rural Development Agency
NABARD	-	National Bank for Agriculture and Rural Development
TAHDCO	-	TamilNadu Adi–Dravidar Housing and Development Corporation

Index